Business Leaders Praise
Ten Action Items for Winning Companies:

"Palubiak touches on all the necessary ingredients for long-term corporate success. He cuts through the clutter and focuses on the essentials that really matter."

Jim Weddle, Managing Partner of Edward Jones
Investment Firm – *edwardjones.com*

"I've read dozens of business books from some of the most revered business leaders and this book provides very clear, simple and actionable principles for successful management. It can serve as an instruction manual for leaders no matter how large or small the company."

Dave Peacock, President, Anheuser-Busch
Worldwide Beverage – *anheuser-busch.com*

"This book is a fast-paced, pragmatic and concise overview of the core operating principals for growing and managing a successful business. Easy and fun to read!"

Dennis Haar, CEO, SS8 Networks
Silicon Valley Technology – *SS8.com*

"What a great read! So often, companies lose sight of the important, common sense approach on running a business. A resource for all companies to practice!"

Steve Schulte, CEO, Porta-King Building Systems
Global Leader – *portaking.com*

"Enjoyed it! Quick read. Lots of good, common sense ideas."

Bill Bay, CEO, Mel Bay Publications
Worldwide Music Publishing – *melbay.com*

"The handbook is a very concise source of common sense tips that will keep a manager or entrepreneur focused on the key issues that drive a successful business. Great job!"

Mike Mooney, Chairman, Footwear Unlimited
International Importer – *footwearunlimited.com*

"What starts out as a book that covers the basics, this quick read reminds even the most successful entrepreneur what it takes to continue to build a fundamentally strong company."

Ray Gadd, CMO, Treasure Valley Foods
Wholesale Food – *treasurevalley.com*

"This is an excellent collection of common sense strategies that can move any company ahead. It covers a lot of ground in a short time that is clear to all levels of management, from the board room to the shop floor."

Greg Sahrmann, COO, Payment Alliance International
ATM Processor – *paymentallianceintl.com*

"Great work! It's a quick read full of management insight. Every leader should constantly review these easy to use tips."

Denny Reed, COO, Momentum Worldwide
International Marketing – *momentumww.com*

"This is a welcome antidote to some very complex, very expensive "panaceas" like ISO, Six Sigma, and the like. It's nice to see a quick, concise tome that brings true high value and common sense into the business vernacular."

Mike Kane, President, VRCG
Automotive Consulting – *vrcg.com*

"This is a quick and practical read. Reminds me of the old axiom that "Common Sense is so Uncommon." As the world moves increasingly faster, this book crystallizes what's most important to gaining and keeping loyal internal and external customers."

Mark Grieman, Executive VP, Adams Gabbert
Technology Consulting – *adamsgabbert.com*

"This is an excellent, practical guide that should be kept out in the open for a quick reference. Good job!"

Rick Allman, CEO, AMS Controls
Global Electronics Integrator – *amscontrols.com*

Printed in the United States of America
10 9 8 7 6 5 4 3 2 1

ISBN: 978-1-893308-13-8

Optim Consulting Group

optimgroupusa.com

St. Louis, Missouri

*Dedicated to Kelly, Steven and Jennifer
as they set forth...*

Table of Contents

Tips

Purpose

The Business Person's Handbook consists of a series of practical tips that address real world issues facing today's business person. The purpose is to provide concise, yet thought-provoking perspectives that will lead to timely, positive solutions for you and your team.

Goal Setting
Company Versus Personal

The role of goal (objective) setting has become significantly more important in all aspects of life during the past few years. We are committed to making ourselves healthier in both mind and body. We want more time with the family than our parents were able to enjoy. We want more time to spend in personal activities such as hobbies, sports, traveling and volunteer work.

At work we strive harder than ever before to outperform the competition while attempting to satisfy our customers' needs. We must offer even better products and services at even lower prices, if we hope to reach our goals of greater market share, revenues and profitability.

Whether it be personally or organizationally related, the value of goal setting has become paramount to one's success. The goal is a quantifiable benchmark that provides a gauge for measuring present and future performance. And it is a stimulus for accomplishment because it offers a sense of purpose.

The proper balance of personal and corporate goals will provide greater harmony and greater opportunity so that all your goals can be realized. You cannot afford to delay, however, because each lost moment or day will result in some form of additional cost to yourself and to your company.

"The future ain't what it used to be."

Yogi Berra

Mission Statement

Management can establish corporate goal(s) at any time for any reason. However, for any goal to serve its true purpose, management must fully understand the goal's intent and implications.

The first step is for management to recognize the difference between a corporate mission statement and the corporate goal. The former is more intangible in nature. It is a "vision" of the future. It should conjure up feelings of excitement and pleasure. It defines why the company exists. It provides direction for the company for years to come. It should be shared internally and externally.

For example, ABC Company's mission may be "to become the leading supplier of computer software systems to non-profit organizations throughout the state."

Corporate Goals

The corporate goal is more concrete than the mission statement. While actually accomplishing the goal should certainly conjure up feelings of excitement and pleasure, the daily movement of working towards the goal is more operational in scope. The goal is more short-term in nature than the mission statement. And it is primarily designed to be shared with employees and shareholders.

Traditionally, corporate goals have related to three primary benchmarks: (1) market share (2) revenues, and (3) profitability. In recent years, customer metrics have been added to the list.

Goals need not be mutually exclusive. Many companies pursue more than one simultaneously. Goals are typically set for time frames ranging between six months to three years. In the case of ABC Company, its six-month goal is to improve customer satisfaction ratings to 90%. The twelve-month goal is to increase revenues by 25% and pre-tax profitability to 15% with a 40% market share.

Personal Goals

While examining corporate goals, management should simultaneously establish and/or review their own personal goals. Frequently, the firm's goals are a mirror of management's personal philosophies.

For instance, ABC's company's president once worked for a firm that required substantial overnight travel. This proved disheartening because he felt cheated from spending cherished time with his family. He vowed never to subject his employees to the same hardship if and when he was in charge. Consequently, he has restricted ABC's geographic growth to the state where the business is located, so that overnight travel will be limited.

When the management team consists of more than one person, the first step in goal setting should entail the completion of individual personality profiles. While general personalities may already be known, an outside facilitator can assist in documenting the specific traits that should be discussed in an open forum. This provides an insight as to why individuals favor different personal and business goals.

The second step is for the facilitator to assist the management team in establishing and/or reviewing personal goals. The group will begin by determining which time frames should be chosen. Ideally, the time frames selected will include short-term (six to twelve months), medium-term (one to three years) and long-term (over three years) goals. Then members should share their goals which are recorded in column form on the left side of a flip chart or chalkboard for each time frame.

Once everyone has identified his or her personal goals, the facilitator will list the business goals in column form on the right side of the flip chart or chalkboard.

The next step is to compare each individual's personal and business goals for each time frame. The partners of a local wholesale distributor shared their goals as follows:

Partner A (Passive Personality)

Time Frame	Personal	Business
6 months	Paint house	Hire assistant
12 months	Join choir 10% salary increase	10% revenue increase 10% profit increase
36 months	Extended vacation Write a book	30% revenue increase 30% profit increase

Partner B (Dominating Personality)

Time Frame	Personal	Business
6 months	Enter MBA program	New computer system
12 months	Hike Australia 20% salary increase	25% revenue increase 20% profit increase
36 months	Buy vacation home Chair association	90% revenue increase 50% profit increase

Resolution

This was the first time in years that the partners had actually shared their personal and business goals. Tremendous tensions had developed among them during this period of time; each of them had felt slighted by the other. Not until they openly discussed their personality types and current goals did they recognize that they were on different paths. Once they had a clear understanding of each other, mutual respect was re-established. They have since unified their efforts in reaching not only their individual goals, but also in working together towards realizing their corporate mission.

Summary

In conclusion, goal (objective) setting is important in all aspects of our lives. Whether it be personally or organizationally related, goal setting is paramount to success. In terms of business, the firm's goals are frequently a mirror of management's personal philosophies. For this reason, it is imperative that management simultaneously establish and/or review their business and personal goals as a team. There is no better way to unify efforts and keep everyone on the same path.

"Do not speak for other men, speak for yourself."

Henry David Thoreau

When Albert Einstein developed the theory of relativity, he referenced the "system of coordinates." He stated that if an individual tossed a stone from on top of a traveling train towards the ground, that person would see the stone drop in a straight line. However, if someone on the ground saw the train passing by as the stone was tossed, that person would actually see the stone drop in the path of a parabola. These paths are derived by connecting the points (coordinates) at which the travelling stone is seen from each individual's perspective. Einstein said that both perspectives were correct.

This concept is no different from that of the personal and business goals held by individuals in a corporation. The goals may be seen from different perspectives, but in reality they may actually be quite similar goals for all parties involved.

Corporate Mission
Why Have One

Close your eyes and envision your dream vacation. Is it exploring the pyramids of Egypt; sailing in the Caribbean; a trip with the family to Disney World; or playing on a sports fantasy team? Whatever your dream might be, it undoubtedly conjures up feelings of excitement and pleasure.

At first the dream may seem hazy. You may not have a clear picture. But the more you place yourself in that dream, the more focused it becomes. And in time, you realize that with the proper motivation and commitment the dream vacation can become a reality.

Your company mission statement is analogous to your dream vacation:

▶ It should represent a "vision" of the future.

▶ It should conjure up feelings of excitement and pleasure.

▶ It should become a well focused picture in your mind.

Your company mission should represent a far-reaching goal that can become reality with the proper motivation and commitment of your unified team.

**"Drive thy business,
or it will drive thee."**

Benjamin Franklin

Are mission statements meaningful? Absolutely, if properly conceived and executed! Otherwise, the mission statement will become a worthless document. It actually can become damaging to the company if it results in negative feelings among the rank and file.

Reasons for Failure

There is no published data that rank by percentage the failure-success level of mission statement utilization. However, there is an endless list of examples that reflect both scenarios. Let's first examine some of the reasons stated for the failure of mission statements, either in design or execution:

Vacuum Syndrome

One of the most common reasons for mission statement failure is that a business owner or a management team develops the mission statement in a vacuum. They decide that having a mission statement would be "cool." However, no effort is made to consider the employees' perspective. Management develops its new revelation in a vacuum, and announces the concept at a staff meeting.

In the vacuum syndrome, management misses the opportunity to gain insights from the rest of the organization. What if employees could have warned management that the entire marketplace was beginning to change, and that this would impact the company mission? What if a marketing person had not yet communicated that the competition had developed a new technology that might make current products obsolete? Or that new environmental laws had unexpectedly created a problem that will force clients away from the company's current product line?

Publication Syndrome

The publication syndrome occurs when the creator(s) of the mission statement are looking to publish a book. The mission statement soon loses purpose as it grows into a novel-length tome. The vision of a dream vacation is no longer a simple picture. The authors include every detail possible. The simple road map becomes an exhaustive itinerary including every road and highway, rest stop, restaurant, tourist activity and sleeping accommodations for the entire vacation.

In the publication syndrome, management loses sight of the mission. In fact, they become wrapped up in details that are irrelevant to the mission. The mission statement should not be complex. It should be easily understood, easy to remember by the entire organization and kept under fifty words in length.

Nearsighted Syndrome

The nearsighted syndrome occurs when management decides that implementing a mission statement will be a great way to quickly motivate the rank and file about some short-term issue. This could be as simple as boosting revenues or profits by the next quarter. Management doesn't care who is involved in the mission's development as long as it is rolled-out promptly.

The problem here is that the mission statement is short-term oriented, rather than long-term oriented. It focuses on next quarter's revenues or profits, and not on the future mission of the organization. The mission statement should never be used as an artificial, short-term motivating device. When it is used for this purpose, negative feedback from the employees is to be expected, particularly if they already feel management is manipulating them.

Impossible Dream Syndrome

The impossible dream syndrome does not limit employee involvement in the creation of the mission statement. It is concise, motivating and well received by the entire team. However, this syndrome goes beyond being "almost" impossible. It is impossible!

The consequence of the impossible dream syndrome is that the mission will quickly be deemed impractical, and apathy will set in. There will be no true motivation for realizing the mission. This occurred when a small manufacturer released the following mission statement after consulting its employees: "We will become the world's largest supplier of industrial valves." Very quickly, the group realized the statement was impractical and, therefore, it held no value for them.

The Right Approach

The mission statement should define why your company exists. Several fundamental questions must be answered:

▶ What is our business?

▶ Who is our customer?

▶ What is our customer's perception of value?

▶ How will our business be shaped in the future?

Management guru Peter Drucker, said that the mission statement should also be shaped by the following five critical factors:

Critical Factors

I. Your company's history of direction and achievements.

Do not shift radically from your company's historical focus unless this strategic choice is necessitated by a major event such as a change in technology, economics, government regulation, demographics, society, or competition.

Example: Although it was late to the party, IBM was eventually forced to accept the personal computer market as a mission reality. Yet today, IBM is no longer a personal computer supplier.

II. The current preference of your company's ownership and management.

Personal preferences of your leadership will obviously have an impact on significant corporate strategy and decisions.

Example: An equipment distributor decided to service only the local marketplace because senior management had no desire to engage in overnight travel.

III. Influences of your market environment.

Threats or opportunities occur that may have an impact on your firm's performance.

Example: The state school system has mandated that on-line education become an integral component of future programs. This presents a wide-open market for new business opportunities.

IV. Limits of your company's resources.

You have a limited amount of time and dollars. You must determine where and how these are to be utilized.

Example: Funds are not available for a regional grocery chain to expand nationally.

V. Your company's distinctive competencies.

Your firm delivers products and/or services which satisfy certain customers' needs. You must maintain focus and not deviate too far from your core strengths.

Example: Enterprise Rent-A-Car could rent computers, but their strength is managing vehicles.

Clear Missions

The following mission statements fulfill the criteria just described:

McDonald's is to be the best quick service restaurant experience. Being the best means providing outstanding quality, service, cleanliness, and value, so that we make every customer in every restaurant smile.

Caterpillar will be the leader in providing the best value in machines, engines and support services for customers dedicated to building the world's infrastructure and developing and transporting its resources. We provide the best value to customers.

Summary

In summary, the mission statement should be as motivating as the "dream vacation." Its creation should include input from all parts of the company team. It should emphasize market rather than product. It should be challenging to attain, but not impossible. It should represent a common thread for management and the employees. It should provide direction for the company for years to come, yet be flexible enough to change as the need arises. It should be shared with customers and prospects. And it should be kept under fifty words in length.

"Think mission before commission."

Mark Victor Hansen

Think Mission *Before* Commission

Know and understand your customer's corporate mission. What is it and what does it mean? And more important, does the organization practice what it preaches?

Answers to these questions will help you assess whether you are spending time with the right customers, and if so, how best to reinforce your position relative to both of your missions. For example: "We provide a quality, valued service as do you our customer. We are a low cost supplier as are you."

Employee Partnership
What Is The Benefit

There has been much talk in recent years about internal and external customers. These discussions indicate that the employee's needs should be recognized as being as important to the organization as that of the ultimate customer.

There seems to be a correlation between those companies who develop partnerships with their employees and those having more satisfied customers. More satisfied customers provide a road map to increased financial success for both the company and its employees.

The late Sam Walton, founder of Wal-Mart, believed his company's phenomenal success was a direct result of how its employees, referred to as associates, are inherently treated within the organization.

Walton preached, "The way management treats the associates is exactly how the associates will then treat the customer. And if the customer is treated well, they will return again and again, and that is where real profits lie, not in trying to drag strangers in for one-time purchases..."

He also believed and advocated that, "Partnership involves money—which is critical to any business relationship—but it also involves basic human consideration, such as respect."

**"If you command wisely,
you'll be obeyed cheerfully."**

Thomas Fuller

Size is Not an Issue

There are three key issues about Sam Walton's "internal customers" or associates.

First, company size and geographic dispersion should not be determinants in establishing a true partnership philosophy throughout your organization.

For example, despite its incredible size and broad geographic dispersion, Wal-Mart has overcome the challenge of dispensing a partnership philosophy throughout its more than two million employee, international organization. Relatively speaking, the smaller-sized business should find the process much easier to execute.

Human Consideration

Second, Walton advocated: that, "Partnership involves money—which is critical to any business relationship—but it also involves basic human consideration, such as respect."

As discussed earlier, the human consideration aspect often has a significant impact on the financial success for both the company and employees. There seems to be a correlation between those companies who develop partnerships with their employees and having more satisfied customers. And more satisfied customers lead to positive results.

The first step in developing a partnership with your employees is to eliminate the traditional "we versus them" attitude, which embraces the hierarchy in so many businesses. Take to heart the following list of recommendations:

▶ Refer to your people by some phrase other than "employees." Know their names. Use empowering descriptions such as associates, partners or team members.

▶ Confirm that your team understands the company mission and goals. They need to know the target before they aim.

▶ Hire people who embrace the `shared vision' attitude. There must be a unified commitment from the entire team.

▶ Let the associates know what is expected of them. They will surprise you with their commitment and ingenuity.

▶ Listen to your associates. Ask them how they can be better served so that they can better serve the customer.

▶ Keep close to your external customers so you know what they desire and how well your team is delivering on that desire.

▶ Inform your associates regularly on their performance. Feedback provides a mechanism for their continuous improvement.

▶ Praise people in public and criticize them in private. Praise should be based on true results or it will not be taken seriously. Criticism should be constructive.

▶ Inform your associates regularly on the company's performance. They need a benchmark to gauge success.

Money Issues

Walton's third issue focuses on the money aspect of the associate partnership. There are numerous financial benefits to be realized from truly nurturing such a relationship.

First, know that if you elect to create a more pleasant work environment for your team, it has been proven that your associates' attitudes will be positively influenced. While it is difficult to measure the specific payback of such an investment, positive attitudes by the team generally translates into greater productivity and profitability.

Second, employee turnover is typically lower in those organizations that empower employees to function as if they were shareholders. This translates into measurable cost savings for your organization due to lower turnover expense. Some examples include the following:

Reduced Turnover Equals Savings

▶ Administrative costs associated with recruiting and hiring will be greatly reduced as turnover slows down.

▶ Management and associates will spend less time in the employee recruiting, interviewing, orientation and training steps.

▶ Learning curves will decrease if fewer positions are vacated and filled by new associates.

▶ Lost knowledge and experience of departing associates will be greatly reduced.

Lost Customers Cost

Unhappy associates can have a major impact on your bottom line. Quite simply, they can and will make your customers unhappy.

Studies, including those done by The Technical Assistance Project (TARP) indicate that 65% of the unhappy customers who quit doing business with a particular company do so for reasons other than poor product or price. Service is considered the overriding factor. In other words, the supplier did a poor job of providing service during some point of the transaction causing the customer to defect.

This becomes an important consideration when one realizes how difficult and expensive it can be to replace lost customers. It is frequently pointed out that the cost of replacing a lost customer is six to nine times as great as it is in keeping a current customer. If only we listened more closely!

Intrapreneurial Partners

Ray Higgins, owner of Fritz's Custard, has taken Sam Walton's partnership philosophy to heart. Higgins attributes the dramatic growth of his small firm to his team of designated "co-workers." These individuals truly feel they are vested in the partnership of the organization because they are empowered to function as if they were shareholders. They flourish within an entrepreneurial environment.

Higgins says, "You need good people to grow. They must run the business as if it were their own. I do not run our facility, but rather, everybody contributes as part of the team."

Throughout the year, Higgins' team receives feedback. The feedback is not a one-time event. It is part of an ongoing process that Higgins has implemented. There is also an annual awards dinner, and, every few years, a team vacation trip.

Summary

Remember what Sam Walton preached? "The way management treats the associates is exactly how the associates will then treat the customers. And if the customers are treated well, they will return again and again, and that is where real profits lie, not in trying to drag strangers in for one-time purchases."

Walton must have known something. He built one of the largest and most successful firms in the world under the partnership concept. Obviously, the internal customer really does matter.

**"Do not wait for extraordinary
circumstances to do good;
try to use ordinary situations."**

Jean Paul Richter

So often in our efforts to satisfy customer needs we seem to bypass one of our greatest assets– that of our employees, our "internal customers."

Whether the employees are referred to as associates, partners or team members, these individuals represent the ultimate link between management and the customer. They are the one component in the value chain that is capable of providing feedback from both the customer, and themselves, on how well your organization is performing in delivering its products and services to the marketplace.

Remember that your business exists to satisfy customers' needs, and that those needs invariably change over time. You must continuously probe to determine where there is pain or passion. These are the two drivers that create a need. When your customer has pain there is a need for relief. And when your customer has passion there is a need to fulfill a desire. In either case, your quick and accurate assessment spells opportunity.

By listening to your associates, you gain firsthand knowledge as to how you are performing in satisfying your customers' needs. These perceptions are critical for the success of your company in realizing its mission and goals.

"Better three hours too soon than a minute too late."

Shakespeare

Feedback Mechanisms

There are numerous methods for staying in touch with your associates. The simplest is to establish an ongoing process for them to share information with management and their fellow team members. As opportunities and issues of concern surface, the associate should be made to feel comfortable in delivering this information within the organization.

The freedom to openly communicate, whether it be via written messages, oral, e-mail or some other method, will ensure that everyone feels their input will be considered.

The ongoing feedback mechanisms can be designed in a free-flowing format, or structured on a more formal basis. For example, written messages, verbal exchanges and e-mail may be used as the associate sees fit. They can be prioritized in such a way that some issues can be discussed spontaneously, while others are addressed on a more formal basis, such as scheduled meeting times.

In addition to this ongoing feedback from associates, a formal audit of their perceptions under the guidance of an outside facilitator can provide valuable information. The focus can be on particular aspects of the organization's performance or be broader in scope.

Known as the employee perception survey, the audit can either be completed by all the associates or by a sampling of those in various parts of the company. This survey has become an integral tool in many a company's quest to gain competitive superiority.

Employee Perception Survey

The intent of the *employee perception survey* is to gain a better understanding of the associates' perceptions about issues known to be important for the smooth and efficient management of the organization. The survey provides feedback regarding those "critical issues" that will produce an accurate picture about where to focus the company's improvement energies as it strives to satisfy its customers and fulfill its own mission and goals.

The survey should be designed to meet the particular needs of any organization. The following sections have proven valuable in covering the core issues affecting most companies:

Section One

The first part of the survey is to ask the associates to rank various issues (usually 20-30) from most important to least important for the long-term success of the firm. These are ranked in a format such as from number 1 (most important) to number 10 (least important). Each number should be used only once. Typical issues include:

▶ Company mission and goals

▶ Company culture and team effort

▶ Rewards and recognition

▶ Product and service quality

The next step is to identify which of the rated issues offer the greatest current opportunity for improvement. Once again, this is based on how the associate perceives the situation.

Section Two

Section two consists of a series of open-ended questions designed specifically for the company. Common among these questions is the issue of how the associates perceive their personal roles relative to the company mission. Of equal importance is the question of what role the associates perceive their superiors play (or should play) within the organization. Questions for this section include:

▶ What is your role within the organization?

▶ Do you fulfill your role?

▶ What is the role of your boss?

▶ Does your boss fulfill the role as described?

▶ How might your roles better assist you both in helping the company realize its mission and goals?

Section Three

The primary purpose of this section is to identify the strengths and weaknesses of the company as perceived by the associates. There are several questions that should be answered here, including the following:

▶ Do the associates agree by department, division and/or universally on the strengths and weaknesses of the company? If not, why?

▶ What can be done to improve the company's performance in satisfying its customers as well as in realizing its mission and goals?

Summary

The employee–associate, partner or team player is the ultimate link between management and the customer. He or she is the one component in the value chain capable of providing feedback from the customer, as well as personal feedback on how well the company is performing.

In summary, the employee perception survey offers an excellent method for gathering this critical information. It should be considered an integral tool for the company in reaching competitive superiority.

"It is no profit to have learned well, if you neglect to do well."

Publilius Syrus

tip 5

The Height of Ingratitude
The Customer

"You are already sharply aware of the phenomenon of the new consumer, because you are one. On behalf of yourself or your company, you are almost certainly a better informed, more demanding, shrewder, and busier buyer than ever before. Now multiply yourself by billions worldwide and you begin to see the scope of what is happening and how it changes the game for every business on earth."

-Marshall Loeb, Retired Editor, Fortune magazine

The customer continues to become "better informed, more demanding, shrewder and busier than ever before." Over the past century, this developmental process has been occurring at an increasingly faster pace in the United States. In the rest of the world it has been happening as well, but at varying speeds.

The ever-accelerating demands of the changing customer profile are not going to slow down, just as you are not going to slow down the demands of your suppliers. Therefore, your company will only succeed in realizing its goals relative to market share, revenues and profitability if it truly understands and meets the ever-changing demands of its customers.

"The secret to business is to know something that nobody else knows."

Aristotle Onassis

Reviewing America's history over the past century-plus will provide some perspective as to how and why the American customer has evolved over time.

Understanding the customer's evolution will enable businesses to become better prepared for marketing both domestically and abroad. There are six distinct periods of time that should be considered:

Production Era (Late 1800s)

Sales Era (Early to Middle 1900s)

Quality Era (1970s)

Marketing Era (1980s)

Customer Focus Era (1990s)

Digital Era (2000s)

Production Era (Late 1800s)

This period was represented by two distinctive customers—the urban city dweller and the rural farmer. In both cases, leisure time was limited due to the need to work long hard hours, often seven days a week, in an effort to generate enough funds to cover the family's basic expenses. Children rarely received education beyond the primary grades; their time was spent as breadwinners. Discretionary income was frequently nonexistent. The family was under-educated, and consequently, not sophisticated as buyers.

Due to the lack of antitrust laws, the marketplace was dominated by monopolies. Therefore, customers had limited selection in many of their purchases. The theme for business was simply to produce the basic products that consumers could afford; that is what they would buy.

This period brought both World War I and World War II. During this time antitrust laws, child labor laws, and collective bargaining laws came into existence. Thanks in part to technology transfers from our military efforts, the customer made great gains as a buyer.

The traditional family was at its peak. While Dad worked, Mom stayed home with the kids. The school system blossomed and everyone had the chance to become educated. Firms began to advertise through the new technologies of the day (radio and television) in an effort to make gains against a host of new competitors.

Companies had to do nothing more than offer an "adequate product." Consumers had money and appetites. They wanted products. Henry Ford's mass production capabilities evidenced technological developments that allowed firms to meet expanding consumer demand. The reward for satisfying the growing demands of the marketplace was unprecedented financial success. The theme was to out-produce and outsell the competition.

Quality Era (1970s)

During the 1970s, it became apparent that something was wrong with the quality of American products. The domestic automotive industry became a focal point of this concern. Consumers came to realize that German and Japanese made cars were of higher quality than those made by Chrysler, Ford and General Motors. In many cases the imports were also less expensive!

The "Quality Movement" began seriously in the United States in the early 1980s when the quality gurus, including Edwards Deming, gained the attention of American manufacturers such as Motorola. They came to recognize that the customer expected high product quality, and that products not meeting those higher expectations were eliminated from consideration by the customer.

Service quality, too, became a key area of concern. The entire process for delivering goods and services; "the how you get it" component, became as critical as "what you get." Firms such as Honda and Disney took the lead.

Marketing Era (1980s)

The Marketing Era was a period when business came to realize that selling alone was not sufficient for success. Business needed a more sophisticated approach to winning over customers. Otherwise, it could not realize the critical goals of increasing market share, revenues and profitability.

It became apparent to companies that the customer and marketplace had to be researched carefully before new products and services were developed. Selling alone was no longer a guaranteed ticket to large payoffs. The customer not only had become educated as a buyer, but also had numerous companies and products from which to choose. Business had to think in terms of not just selling the product, but also in terms of learning what the marketplace really wanted before going into production.

Customer Focus Era (1990s)

The 1990s brought the era of the "tough new consumer," and the principle of demanding more ...and getting it! As we have seen, Marshall Loeb, Retired Editor of *Fortune* magazine, captured this era perfectly when he stated, *"You are almost certainly a better informed, more demanding, shrewder, and busier buyer than ever before."*

This change placed a new burden on businesses if they expected to remain competitive in any market. The winners learned that they must work in partnership with the buyer regardless of whether that buyer was a consumer or represented an organization. Businesses could only succeed if they understood and anticipated the ever-changing needs and demands of the marketplace. They had to be immersed in a customer-focused philosophy if they expected to surpass the competition.

As we consider the task of becoming customer-focused, it is helpful to review some of the research reports produced by organizations such as the Technical Assistance Research Project. Some key findings from this research follow;

▶ Companies that focus on delivering superior service are able to command higher prices and, ultimately, realize higher profits, greater sales volume growth, and greater market share growth than their competitors.

▶ 96% of unhappy customers never complain to the supplying company about their poor service.

▶ Every dissatisfied customer will share his story with at least nine other people.

▶ 60 - 90% of the customers who are dissatisfied with the service they receive will never return.

Digital Era (2000s)

The much-hyped Y2K scare prior to the turn of the second millennium resulted, not in disaster, but in a global explosion of information technology. Thereafter, the norm for doing business was to be radically and frequently changed, and on short notice as the usage of the internet, web, digital imaging, social networks and other creations captured the imagination, and the pocketbooks, of the masses.

Customers could now be reached instantaneously and they could similarly reach out to suppliers of products and/or services. E-marketing, e-sales, and on-line sourcing through such entities as ebay and amazon.com resulted in a paradigm shift in how the customer was to be marketed and sold. And the paradigm is changing almost daily in some sectors by social media tools such as Facebook and Twitter.

Summary

In conclusion, the customer-focused company delivers not only a quality product and quality service, but also stays in close contact with its customers. The customer-focused company maintains an ongoing partnership with the tough new customer, a partnership that must be continuously nurtured.

"Keep up appearances, whatever you do."

Charles Dickens

The Height of Ingratitude

A man lost his job. After six months he was still jobless and had used up his entire savings. He desperately needed $1,000. His minister said to pray, but he got no results. So he decided to go direct to the Lord. He wrote a tearful letter asking for $1,000. He addressed the letter to God and mailed it stampless.

The postman, thinking it was a child's letter, opened it. After reading it, he was deeply touched and took it that night to his Rotary meeting. They immediately drained their treasury of $250, and then emptied their pockets collecting $250 more. They proudly sent the $500.

A few days later, the postman found another letter like the first. He opened it and read: *God, thanks for the money, but please next time, send it to the United Way, because the Rotary stole half of it!*

Yes, sometimes it is very difficult to satisfy the demanding customer. So where do you begin?

Learning to Read the Need
Equals Dollars

The customers of the last decade would not recognize the customers of today. Today's customers are more sophisticated, more informed, more discriminating, more value-conscious, less tolerant and have less time. They are profoundly aware that they have more choices, and are less loyal to brands and companies. They have real power and they are not afraid to leverage it to get what they want.

Competitors have changed, too. As they keep pace with the ever-changing, more demanding face of the new customer, they recognize that to remain competitive, they too must evolve as the customer evolves. They must continuously refine their offering as the customer's concept of value changes. Just as important, they must be able to deliver to this new customer while producing a consistent profit.

Competing today demands that companies think strategically. Strategy at its essence is the ability to deliver on the customer's concept of value. This is much more difficult than it appears. In today's volatile, ever-changing environment, companies will always be shooting at a moving target. Customer desires will be forever changing.

"You may be a disappointment if you fail, but you are doomed if you don't try."

Aristotle Onassis

Learn to Read the Need

Most companies are not equipped to take care of the new customer. They are still working off the old mental models of customers who have long since disappeared. They do not know what the new customers expect or their demands, but they assume that they do.

As customer expectations change and the bar is raised, companies suddenly begin losing ground and they don't know why. The customer continues to evolve, and demands more and different things. The ability to deliver wanes, the gap widens and the decline accelerates. It becomes apparent that the old business strategy has stopped working.

Companies do not have a choice anymore. They must identify the customers they are best equipped to serve, and then continue reinventing their business to meet the needs of that specific subset of customers. Companies who are not focused on their customers will go out of business. Gut feelings will not work anymore!

The dialogue with the customer must never end. The relationship must be truly interactive. Every product, every service and every activity within the company must deliver something of value that the customer can easily recognize and experience. To accomplish this, new and more sophisticated means must be employed to stay in touch with the customer.

Companies are using focus groups, various survey mechanisms, telephones, internet communications, twitter and even MP3s to listen to the voice of the customer. Front-line employees are being trained to listen to the customer so that they are better equipped to solve the customer's problems.

Selling isn't selling any more. The company must use its customer contact employees as a conduit to the mind of the customer. Every nuance of change in customer attitude must be heard throughout the company. New product and service offerings must be inspired and designed with direct input from the customer.

By design, this new type of constant interaction with the customer must produce two simultaneous results:

1. Components of the business offering that no longer deliver value to the customer must be allowed to atrophy and die. The decline phase of the product life cycle should receive as much attention as the introduction phase.

2. New product and service offerings must be allowed to take shape as business opportunities become apparent.

Continuous reallocation of resources must take place to deliver value that will meet the needs of the new customer.

Focus on the Right Issues

Most "customer satisfaction" surveys ask the customer to gauge the level of performance that is being delivered by the supplier. Customers are asked to rate performance regarding a specific issue, from poor to excellent. For example, a firm might ask its customers to rate their performance in delivering products on time. The survey results are used to focus improvements in those deliverables that the customer has rated poorly.

The presumption here is that companies know which issues are important to the customer. Yet if the customers rate performance "exceptional" for those issues that they care least about, check "below average" for those issues that are more important, and have no option at all for communicating about the issues that they care most about, the survey results can be quite misleading!

A company might review the results and assume that since they did well on nine out of ten issues that "all is well." They fail to realize that the tenth issue might be the most important to the customer, or that the most important issue might not be on the list at all!

On the other hand, when the customer is asked to weigh the issues according to their own hierarchy of values, then the supplier can gain some insights about where to focus the corporate energies and resources. Feedback from customers must always be gathered in two critical dimensions:

1. How IMPORTANT is the issue?

2. How are we PERFORMING regarding the issue?

Using this approach, the supplier can focus on those core issues where the customer places the most value. The value-performance grid is a simple tool that can be used to graphically portray those results.

The value-performance grid allows the customer to provide a "weighting" factor for those issues that they value most. The responsive competitor will allocate the bulk of the company resources to improve performance for those highly valued issues rated as important by the customer, yet where performance is lagging (quadrant D). They will also minimize resource allocation to those issues that are not as important to the customer, despite performance levels (quadrant A and C).

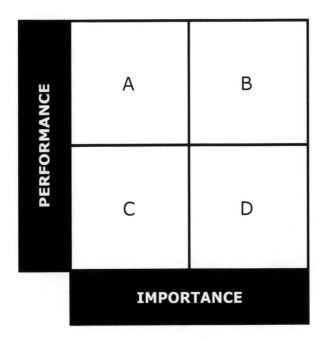

The value-performance grid encompasses a third dimension. That is the cost associated with delivering value issues. Company resource allocation is dependent on the breadth of resources available to the company including such items as time and finances. These factors must be weighed in terms of availability, return-on-investment (ROI) and other modeling practices utilized by the company.

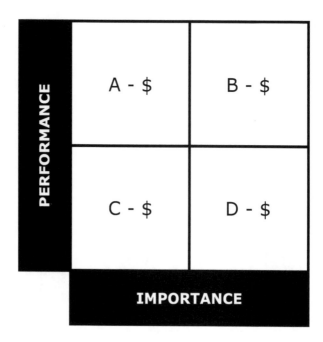

Summary

Staying in constant contact with the customer is critical. Gathering the right kind of information will ensure that strategic planning is fruitful. Every plan must begin and end with the customer in mind. As customers evolve and change, the critical issues will evolve and change. Companies that are truly customer-focused must maintain a high degree of flexibility and responsiveness to change.

"The value is to be determined."

RCP

Competitive Intelligence
Your Enemies

As you read these words, you can rest assured that the competition is busy searching for your faults, and for one simple reason—they want to sneak between the cracks and steal away your customers. Their ultimate goal is to grow and prosper, and if they damage you or put you out of business in the process, that's too bad.

This situation is further complicated because corporate restructuring and downsizing have caused an incredible fragmentation of industry. More jobs than ever before are being taken out of companies and being sub-contracted, adding to an already high proliferation rate of new companies. In total, it is estimated that nearly 1,500 new businesses are being started each day, or roughly 500,000 per year.

The Internal Revenue Service says there are over twenty million companies in the United States. By Federal government definition, only 15,000 of these are considered large businesses, meaning they meet the parameter of employing at least 500 people. These firms represent less than 1% of all firms in the country. Furthermore, about 90% of all U.S. firms have less than twenty employees.

In short, there are a lot of companies out there that are competing to be successful; many of which are striving to be successful at your expense.

"Don't think there are no crocodiles because the water is calm."

Malayan proverb

The competition is out there and they want your customers. If you become complacent or overconfident, they will succeed. On the plus side, they will help push you to new levels of performance and drive you to go forward.

Use competition to your advantage. Accept that they are visiting with your customers on a regular basis. This is not a sign of disloyalty, but rather of intelligence on the part of your customers. They need to garner all the weapons and knowledge available to battle in their industry, just as you do in yours. So, stay close and learn from your customers what tools the competition are providing. Whoever does a better job of reading the needs of customers will have the upper hand in offering a solution.

Competitive Intelligence

The first step in surpassing the competition is to know and to understand them. This is accomplished by collecting *competitive information*. It is important that you begin by recognizing the ethical and legal issues that you may face when collecting and using the information. These issues arise from the following areas:

▶ What type of information are you trying to collect?

▶ How is the information to be obtained?

▶ How is the information to be used?

There are no simple guidelines that define the ethical and legal aspects of collecting competitive information. Perhaps the best approach is to begin by asking yourself, "If my competitors used the same method to collect information on me would I feel injured or slighted?" If you can honesty answer no, then you are favorably positioned to move forward.

Collection Timing

Competitive information can be collected on a continuous basis or when needed for specific purposes. Many firms do both.

An example of collecting continuous information is well-represented by the local grocery store chain that monitors its competitors' prices daily so that it can quickly adjust its own prices accordingly.

In the second case, the grocery chain may need competitive information for a specific purpose. For instance, if the chain is contemplating expanding into a new part of town, it will be beneficial to know what the competition is currently doing in that part of town, as well as how the competition will react if the chain moves into its territory.

Whether competitive information is collected continuously or as needed for a specific purpose, there are several questions which need to be answered. These include:

▶ What is the potential threat of new competitors in the products and markets we are currently serving? What competitive threat exists for those markets that we would like to serve in the future?

▶ What are our suppliers' plans? Will they become our competitor in the future? Or will we become their competitor by integrating backwards?

▶ What are our clients' plans? Will they become our competitor in the future? Or will we become their competitor by integrating forward?

▶ What potential threat exists from substitute products and services? Are our products and services at risk of being replaced by substitutes?

Collecting competitive information is best accomplished when a strategy is formulated before the collection process is initiated. The plan need not be complicated, but it should be comprehensive in nature. It should be very clear in terms of its stated purpose and goals. The individuals responsible for the collection process should understand their roles, and the time lines to which they are to adhere.

The actual sources for competitive information may vary by company and industry. However, there are several sources that should be considered by any firm undertaking a competitive analysis. These include the following:

Information Sources

▶ Employees are frequently an excellent source for competitive information, as well as for designing the competitive analysis. They often have firsthand knowledge of the marketplace, and can provide valuable insights.

▶ Customers will share marketplace information with you, if you have a strong relationship and they feel that you will use it to better serve their needs.

▶ Prospects are frequently looking for better options. If asked properly, they will share with you the products and services which are available in the marketplace, and their opinion of the suppliers.

▶ Lost clients will sometimes divulge why they left you, and what they are getting from the competition.

▶ Industry sources such as trade association publications, industry listings, credit services (Dunn & Bradstreet) and even the Yellow Pages can provide valuable input.

▶ Government publications are broadly available, including such sources as the U.S. Department of Commerce.

▶ Competition often shares substantial information about itself during its promotion and sales efforts. Public relations campaigns, advertising and trade shows are excellent sources of current information.

▶ Although there are numerous sources available for collecting competitive information, the ones listed above should be considered closely.

Information Use

The manner in which the collected competitive information is used is perhaps the most critical issue when undertaking competitive intelligence.

Obviously, the information should be used in an ethical and legal manner. Of equal importance is that the information should be disseminated throughout the organization on a timely basis so that your team is well prepared to understand and take on the competition.

You should compare your company's strengths and weaknesses with that of the competition. You should discuss what changes need to be made for your firm to continue enjoying its success or what you must do to become successful.

The competition is out there, and they want your customers. If you become complacent or overconfident, they will succeed. On the plus side, they will help push you to new levels of performance. They will drive you to go forward. If you find a way to use them to your advantage, you will surely outperform them.

**"Observe your enemies,
for they first find your faults."**

Antisthenes

The marketplace of today is dramatically different from that of even the recent past. The rate of change is accelerating—in industry, in technology, and even the customer is changing. The only way for a business to survive is to keep pace with the change. The only way to succeed is to surpass your competition in the race. Even better is to create your own race, and leave the competition in the dust.

The facts are staggering. Fifty percent (50%) of the companies on the Fortune 500 list in 1980 no longer exist. Entire markets, such as the airline industry, have been hit broadside. Full service carriers, Pan American and Eastern Airlines, for example, have been replaced by the likes of Southwest Airlines whose strategy is to provide a low-cost, low-frills package. Another example is the explosion of technology arising as a result of the personal computer.

Leading the pack is software giant Microsoft, which has skyrocketed on the Fortune 500 list while practically developing an industry of its own. Children of all ages use Microsoft products for entertainment and school projects. Simultaneously, their parents use the software packages for both personal use and business purposes.

Reviewing the Fortune 500 list indicates that American business has changed significantly in terms of markets and companies over the past few years. The impact on the corporate life cycle has been substantial. No longer can a company expect to survive if it does not keep up with its competition. It must recognize that the threat of competition extends well beyond those that it competes with today. This includes new entrants into the marketplace and substitute products, as well as those you least expect—your suppliers and even your clients.

**"Do not invest your whole life
in one hope."**

Austin O'Malley

Creating Your Own Race

Monitor Your Offering

The first step in creating your own race is to continuously monitor your current product and service offering. Are they satisfying the needs of your customers? Whether it is daily, monthly, quarterly or annually, you must compare the results with your corporate goals. When the goals for market share, revenues or profits have been met or exceeded, you may consider yourself fortunate to have a short-term competitive advantage. However, this does not bring long-term guarantees and is not a justification for complacency; if you have not reached your goals, the need for action is even more urgent.

Growth Strategies

The second step in creating your own race is to focus on new business opportunities—known as growth strategies. The key is to evaluate them relative to market share, revenue and profit potential. Intensive growth, the first strategy type, represents growth within your company's current line of business. The second growth strategy is integrative growth, which is to build or acquire business(s) and/or product(s) within your company's current business line. And the third is diversification, or adding unrelated business(s) and/or product(s).

Growth Strategies
Intensive Growth Integrative Growth Diversification Growth

Intensive Growth has been used by Apple as they have *penetrated* outside of their original personal computer market by expanding sales within the education and graphic sectors. They have further *developed* their market by creating a direct distribution channel with the highly successful Apple Store. *Product development* has also increased the revenue and profit stream through the addition of the iPhone, iPod and iPad.

Intensive Growth
Market Penetration
Market Development
Product Development

Integrative Growth

Integrative Growth has long been practiced by the automobile manufacturers. General Motors first began *backward integration* by purchasing and building its own component suppliers. However, *forward integration* has been limited because General Motor's vehicles are sold through its network of independent dealerships, which it does not own. *Horizontal integration* occurred when General Motors originally purchased several competing manufacturers, giving it a broad product line, which included Buick, Chevrolet, Oldsmobile and Cadillac.

Integrative Growth

Backward Integration
Forward Integration
Horizontal Integration

Diversification Growth

Diversification Growth is used by the direct marketing computer companies such as Dell. The *concentric strategy* occurred with the addition of the laptop computer to their product line, which appeals to current clients as well as many first-time buyers. *Horizontal diversification* involves offering new unrelated technologies to current clients. Dell could accomplish this by offering products such as portable radios and electric shavers. Alternatively, they might seek *conglomerate diversification*, which involves the purchase of businesses that have no relationship to their current industry, technology, or clients.

Diversification Growth
Concentric Diversification
Horizontal Diversification
Conglomerate Diversification

Selecting the Race Strategy

The approach for selecting the proper race strategy may be accidental or deliberate. By many accounts, 3M Corporation's *market development* success with the Post-it Note was purely accidental. One of the co-inventors was actually developing a light adhesive for sticking a paper marker in his song book during church services. Little did he realize the value of his invention at the time.

On the other hand, management expert Michael Porter advocates a very structured process for analyzing the marketplace. The intent is to minimize the risks and maximize the potential payback. In a structured approach, Porter says you need to properly answer and respond to the following critical questions:

Critical Questions

▶ What are our core competencies (strengths) and weaknesses? Should these guide our decisions or can we adapt to any opportunity?

▶ What is our competition doing? What are their plans? And how will they react to ours?

▶ What is the potential threat of competitors in the products and markets we are exploring?

▶ What are our suppliers' plans? And how will they react to ours?

▶ What are our clients' plans? And how will they react to ours?

▶ What potential threat exists from substitute products and services?

Summary

By properly responding to Michael Porter's questions, Southwest Airlines is an example of a company that has successfully implemented an intensive growth strategy. Southwest understands that its core competence (strength) is to provide low-cost, low-frills air transportation between cities of close proximity (about 300 miles). While the full-service airlines are struggling to compete against Southwest, the airline continues to focus on market penetration as it strategically expands geographically throughout the nation.

Due to its high quality of service, new entrants to the market have been unable to take away Southwest's satisfied client base.

Perhaps the greatest threat to Southwest is the commercial bus and train. They may become transportation substitutes if Southwest's prices are driven too high by their suppliers of such items as planes, fuel and labor. Yet, Southwest's goal of being the lowest-priced form of transportation between its targeted cities may prevent this marketing myopia.

**"Hit the ball over the fence,
then you can take your time
going around the bases."**

John Raper

The Endless Race

The rate of change in the marketplace is not going to diminish; if anything, it will actually continue to accelerate. Consequently, the race of business is not going to end. Competitors will come and go, as will industries, technologies and clients. The only way to survive is to keep pace. And the only way to succeed is to surpass your competition in the race by strategically out-maneuvering them.

Product Offering
Where to Start

In recent years, management has frantically responded to shareholder pressures by attempting to improve financial performance through such approaches as corporate downsizing, restructuring and reengineering. General Motors and IBM are two examples of companies that have scrambled to implement these approaches in an effort to reach acceptable business goals. In many instances, they are performing late-stage surgery due to their negligence in not treating the illnesses earlier.

Companies will not be competitive in today's dynamic marketplace unless the fundamentals are in place. These provide the baseline for producing quality products in the most efficient and cost-effective manner possible. Anything less will not enable companies to satisfy customer demands. And without satisfied customers, a business cannot expect to survive, much less prosper.

While the fundamentals are being implemented, you must also concentrate your efforts on analyzing your current product/service portfolio. Many questions need to be answered, such as: What is your current offering? How well does it satisfy your customers' needs? What other customers might it satisfy? Is it consistent with your corporate mission? How does it contribute to reaching your corporate goals?

"We always change, renew, rejuvenate ourselves, otherwise we harden."

Goethe

Continuous Portfolio Analysis

The practice of monitoring your product/service portfolio is analogous to a coach who must continuously review the team. The first step toward winning the championship requires the coach to **evaluate** whether or not the team has the right combination of players for the competitive strategy. If not, the coach must **eliminate and/or recruit** specific players. The third step is to **modify** the game plan as needed. And finally, the coach must quantify the **results** on the big day.

In reviewing the team, the coach must be conscious of both internal and external factors. The former includes items such as the quality of the team's training facility, the strengths and weaknesses of the players and assistant coaches, and the support level of the team's fans. The external factors include the competition's players, coaches and fans.

The outcome of the championship game will indicate which one of the teams truly has a competitive advantage. Yet, this pertains only to the current season. Regardless of who wins, the coach must continue to review the team if he hopes to have a chance to win the championship next season.

Like the team, no company is exempt from the need to continuously monitor its product/service portfolio. Small and large companies alike have been caught off-guard. For instance, many local barbers that have not updated their services have lost clients to hair stylists. General Motors lost significant revenues to the Japanese when auto buyers became dissatisfied with the GM product line. And IBM was scarred when buyers elected the personal computer (PC) as an alternative to the mainframe.

Just as the coach considers the team's internal factors, so should management when it begins to review the product/service offering. The company mission statement is the starting point. Is it current in describing why the company exists, what is the company's business, and who is the customer?

The corporate goals should be reviewed next. Are they acceptable as well as attainable? Should revenues, profitability and/or market share be the focal point?

Once the big picture items have been considered, management should concentrate on **evaluating** the product portfolio itself. Is the marketing mix appropriate? Are the product, price, promotion and distribution (place) channels appropriate?

The employees are an integral component in this phase. They should be surveyed both formally and informally. The purpose of this input is to gain their perceptions on how well the client base is being served with the current product offering. Are the products meeting expectations? If not, why? Who else might be a prospect for the offering?

The second part of the internal factor evaluation phase is to survey customers. Once again, this should be done both formally and informally. What are the customers' perceptions? Are their needs being fulfilled by the product offering? If not, why? What would it take?

And lastly, non-customers should be interviewed. Why are they not purchasing the product offering? What do they like or not like about it? How are their needs currently being met?

After completing the team evaluation, the coach will **eliminate and/or recruit** the appropriate players in the effort to build a winning team. Once management has completed its evaluation, it must take similar action. There are four primary strategic options pertaining to the product/service offering:

1. *Build* by adding more offerings.

2. *Maintain* by making no changes.

3. *Harvest* the pickings but do not reinvest.

4. *Divest* by selling or dropping the offering.

Known for continuously monitoring its product/service portfolio, McDonald's routinely uses several of the above options.

For example, McDonald's has built upon its original menu by adding such items as the Big Mac and Quarter Pounder. During pilot programs, it frequently harvests products. When the product is well received, it is added to the menu. If not, there is no reinvestment as inventories are depleted. And periodically it will divest products. This happened when it opened McDonald's Express. The menu offering was less than at their traditional restaurant locations and could not compete as a stand-alone building.

Strategic Game Plan

The firm's game plan is similar to the coach's in that both are affected by internal and external factors. As McDonald's continues to review its mission, goals and product/service offering, it must also monitor the external factors. Key issues for McDonald's involve the economy, competition, social issues, political forces and technology. Who, what, where, when and how will these be impactful?

McDonald's must be prepared to **modify** its strategy at any time during the game as the external factors change. Its competitive strategy can take numerous forms. Perhaps best known are the three proposed by Michael Porter:

1. "Overall cost leadership," which means being the lowest cost producer.

2. "Differentiation," which means quality, service or innovation leadership in the product/service offering.

3. "Focus," which means serving in particular niche markets.

Porter argues that a business must fall into one of these categories or it will become caught in the middle and, ultimately, die.

McDonald's is primarily a "low cost producer," that has "differentiated" itself by providing consistent quality food and service. It has modified its strategic game plan to battle new entrants into the market such as Checkers and Rally's. These drive-through competitors have defined a niche market that focuses on clients who accept a limited menu in return for "very" quick service at bargain prices. The McDonald's Express was part of McDonald's modified strategy to combat this effort. However, McDonald's eventually moved away from the Express roll-out due to changing competitive issues.

Summary

The coach can determine the team's progress and modify the strategy throughout the game based on the score. Business has the same opportunity. Whether it be monthly, quarterly or annually, management is able to compare **results** with the corporate goals. When the goals have been met or exceeded, management can assume it truly has a competitive advantage. However, this advantage pertains only to the current season. The product/service portfolio review process must continue if management hopes to have a chance for being the winner again next year.

**"If things seem under control,
you are not going fast enough."**

Mario Andretti

CUSTOMERization
Customer Selection

CUSTOMERization means identifying and serving what you perceive as your optimal customers. By doing such, you become a more successful supplier, and are naturally eager to keep your select customer base satisfied. Your customers will come to think of their relationship with you as a positive experience, and not just as a series of transactions. They will consider you a value source.

The simple fact of business is that all customers are not created equal, but that they should perceive that they are and treated as such. As we have seen, the widely acclaimed Technical Assistance Research Project studies discovered what happens when customers are not well treated:

▶ 65% of customers defect not because of price or product, but rather because of poor service.

▶ Dissatisfied customers will tell from nine to twenty persons about their disenchantment.

The benefit of a satisfied customer base is that people who buy from you will be receptive to your company gaining a greater *share-of-customer*. In other words, they will allow you to do more business with them, and more willing to pay a premium for that opportunity.

You also will be freed from spending a significant portion of your time chasing new prospects to replace those you lost. You will even find that your satisfied customers will openly spread the word about the pleasure of doing business with your company.

"Be civil to all; sociable to many; familiar with few; friend to one; enemy to none."

Benjamin Franklin

Treat All Customers Equally

Employees need to understand the value and importance of treating all customers equally with a 100% service level. The point is worth repeating: If a customer is not satisfied with their service, that customer will share their negative experience with nine to twenty others. This can cause tremendous turmoil in the marketplace.

Even though all customers should be *treated equally*, management must understand that all customers are *not created equal*. In terms of pure return on investment (ROI), some clients will require more time and dollar investment than they will ever give in return.

The first step is to recognize the need to have a targeted portfolio of optimal customers, which includes both short-term and long-term customers.

The short-term customer provides current marketplace feedback, referrals and positive word-of-mouth. The investment required to attract them is limited, and the payoff is great. Since the value of these customers is not perceived as long-term, no effort is made to solicit them as such until their potential changes.

On the other hand, the long-term customer should be targeted with sufficient investment in terms of time and money in an effort to attract and maintain them for life, or for an extended period of time.

How to Target?

The second step is to develop a framework for analyzing your current customer base. The following factors provide a general guideline:

Review your company mission and goals with the rank and file. Be sure there is a consensus. For example, ABC Company's mission is to be the leading supplier of quality coffee products to commercial users in the metropolitan area. The goal is to gain 40% of the market share, and maintain a 15% pre-tax profitability.

Analyze the current customer-base activity by product category. What type and quantities have been purchased over designated time frames? These will vary by company and industry. For instance, ABC Company may decide to focus on various types of coffee purchased over the past twelve months.

Determine the profit contribution per client by product category during the designated time frame. In the case of ABC, over the past twelve months 25% of the client base purchased 65% of the highest margin coffee category. The middle 50% of the client base purchased 30% of the high margin category, and the bottom 25% purchased 5% of it.

NOTE: *This phase of the analysis will only work if you have implemented an accurate pricing and accounting system.*

Compare the results of the profit contribution analysis to your stated company mission and goals. Are they consistent? ABC may have 60% market share, but the pre-tax profitability is only 8%. Is it possible to reach 15% pre-tax profitability at this market share level? ABC needs to clarify its goals and determine whether or not they are compatible with each other. If not, they need to be modified.

Current Customers

The third step is to develop a promotion mix strategy that will focus on gaining more business from existing customers (*share-of-customer*), and help eliminate unwanted customers. But be very careful in its execution. Remember what the studies found? Don't reduce your service level; just be more discriminatory in your promotional campaign so that the right type of customers are repetitively attracted.

For example, ABC Company might increase its direct selling effort to those customers who are prospects for purchasing additional high-profit products. Furthermore, ABC might discontinue marketing to businesses that have purchased nothing but small quantities of discounted products over the past twelve months.

The final step is to target the promotion mix strategy beyond current customers and towards new qualified prospects. Keep in mind that there are two types of customers; short-term and long-term. Therefore, you should determine beforehand which type of prospects you wish to recruit and why! Is their purpose to provide current marketplace feedback, referrals or positive word-of-mouth? Or is their purpose to become lifetime customers?

Lifetime Customer Value

The true customer for life provides both indirect and direct values. The indirect value promotes:

▶ Continuity of client presence that represents company stability in the minds of your employees.

▶ Positive word-of-mouth by the client that will serve a public relations role.

▶ Family belonging where the client feels a paternal need to help you succeed.

The direct value can be measured in both a linear and exponential manner. Carl Sewell references the linear approach in his book, *Customers for Life*. He states that on average, a customer who buys one of his $25,000 automobiles represents a lifetime potential of purchases equal to $332,000. His rationale is that the customer will not only buy another eleven cars during their lifetime, but will also spend $32,000 on parts and service.

The neighborhood grocery store provides another example for determining the lifetime value of a customer. Current studies estimate that the average family of two spends $500 a month on groceries. This equates to $6,000 a year, and $120,000 over twenty years.

The exponential approach will increase the $120,000 grocery store figure dramatically. The first factor to consider is the additional cost of replacing lost customers due to dissatisfaction. Several studies indicate that it costs as much as five times to replace a client as it does to maintain the client. The second factor is the time value of money. Depending on the rate of inflation, $120,000 can actually represent several hundred thousand dollars!

In summary, all customers should be treated with a 100% service level. Your employees need to understand the value and importance of such delivery. However, all clients are not created equal. You have a responsibility to yourself and the company to develop a promotional mix strategy that will enable you to attract the type of customer you will want to have for life.

▶ Treat all customers equally.

▶ Not all are created equal.

▶ Identify optimal customers.

▶ Maximize share-of-customer.

▶ Create an experience, not merely a transaction.

"Always be nice to people on the way up, because you'll meet the same people on the way down."

Wilson Mizner

R. Craig Palubiak is the founder of Optim Consulting Group, a management consulting firm that specializes in facilitating business and growth strategies. His clients range from small privately owned to Fortune 500 companies.

Craig has been a business owner (two national firms) and a corporate executive with Enterprise Rent-A-Car where under his guidance commercial leasing became the first national division. He is a noted author, professional speaker and an adjunct professor.

optimgroupusa.com

cpalubiak@optimgroupusa.com

Notes

Notes

16210106R00079

Made in the USA
Charleston, SC
09 December 2012